POET
SHORT STORIES BY A
BIPOLAR GIRL

MELISSA BURKE

outskirtspress
DENVER, COLORADO

Poetry and Short Stories by a Bipolar Girl
All Rights Reserved.
Copyright © 2012 Melissa Burke
v1.0

Outskirts Press, Inc.
http://www.outskirtspress.com

ISBN: 978-1-4787-2022-5

Outskirts Press and the "OP" logo are trademarks belonging to Outskirts Press, Inc.

PRINTED IN THE UNITED STATES OF AMERICA

Table of Contents

Prologue

All I am is a twenty year old girl (I still consider myself a girl, though technically I have reached womanhood). But am I JUST that? No, I'm much more. I am a "crazy" girl with bipolar disorder, depression, obsessive compulsive disorder, anxiety and an eating disorder. I've been dealing with it pretty much my whole life, but I started actually suffering as it got worse in the eighth grade, at age 13.

"So what?" you might ask. I could have just gotten help and become stable years ago. But I didn't do that. I didn't take the opportunity to get help when it was right in front of my face and I waited until the end of my freshman year in college to say anything and to do anything about it. After all my self-harm, drinking, drugs, cigarettes, etc. I finally decided to do something about all I had endured.

To this day I have been hospitalized three times and have gone to a partial hospital four times, all for my mental health problems. I now see a therapist and a psychiatrist and am on four different meds (for now).

These upcoming poems and short stories will tell it all for you. They're in no specific order (some could be from ninth grade and some could be from a few months ago) and they pretty much tell my story by themselves. So sit back, flip the page and enjoy the ramblings of a bipolar girl.

Simple as That

I have so much built up inside me that I don't even know what I'm hiding anymore. There's so much pain… and for some reason right now, right at this very moment, I feel like I need to let it all out. But that's the problem. I don't know how. I don't know *what*, either.

Even as I sit here, alone, next to my sister's empty bed, hearing the rain gently pattering against the window; Even as I just sit limply on my bed, listening through the silence of the house for any movement; Even as I sit, staring at my phone, letting guilt wash over me; Even as I sit, watching and waiting, 11:28 on a Friday night—my mind is racing. My mind is racing with everything that hurts me, everything I need to rid myself of.

So why is it that I can't find a single thing to say?

Why is it that, though with all my heart I wish to finally let everything out, I can't find a single thing to say?

I feel like all the words are jumbled in a giant orb of sensation in my mind. I feel like maybe it is impossible to put words to things that hurt the most. But then how am I supposed to rid myself of them? I have to at least *try*. But I don't even know where to start.

Perhaps there is no beginning. I can't look for a beginning or end to my trail of hurt. I just have to let it flow out on its own, right? So why is it so hard?

Maybe if I just go by what comes to mind first. Maybe everything will release itself eventually that way.

It's just a letter. A simple fucking letter. I don't get it. Read, comprehend, respond. When has it ever been any more difficult than that?

But I can't bring myself to do it — it hurts too much. So I just sit here and stare at the small portion of the envelope I can see sticking out. I'm tempted to go grab it and read it. Again. But then I'll want to respond. Then I'll realize I can't. Why? Because it hurts. It hurts so goddamn much. I think of all the things I could say. All the things I *should* say. How disappointed I am. How worried. How scared. Say "come back" and "I love you" and "I'm always here." It's so simple. But I can't bring myself to do it.

Instead I am staring at that envelope, 11:44 on a Friday night, and trying to remember. I am trying to remember all the great times, the memories. Her voice. Her face. Her personality. But I can't.

Either my past is deteriorating or she is dead to me.

That is the first time I've admitted that. And both options hurt. A lot.

My past does seem to be deteriorating. I am remembering less and less. The memories are becoming less vivid and no matter how much I search my mind, I can't find them. The memories. Years... *years* are gone. Chunks of life have been stolen away. My past is deteriorating.

She is dead to me. I hurt her. And she hurt me. But we dealt. Then she left. Or maybe I'm the one who left. But we are gone. She is gone. She is dead to me.

But how can she be? If I feel the hurt so much, she is very much alive to me.

If I feel the hurt this much, then there's not much else I can do except write that letter.

After all, it's just a letter. A simple fucking letter, right?

11:55 on a Friday night and I feel guilty.

He texted back, four minutes ago.

Five words, that's all. But each word hurt. Why? This I don't understand. Five simple words. But they felt harsh. Five fucking words. And somehow I feel so much hidden underneath the surface.

Why is it that he makes me feel like I'm the guilty one? When I'm nothing but a puppet.

He is messing up. *He* is doing the hurting. But he makes me feel guilty. Even now I feel guilt for blaming him for this guilt.

I am merely a puppet. But a few kind words and I eagerly crawl back to him. Why? Because I love him. Is that reason enough to let him hurt me? I guess so.

I choose. I have to debate and choose every time. Why do I always choose the hurt?

I love him. But five words. Five simple words. And I hurt.

A fear and a sadness are overtaking me. Why? Because I am tired. Simple as that, I need sleep. I fear that when I wake up I will not be as willing to open myself like this. I fear I will not be able to do it.

And I am sad. Sad that my exhaustion alters the

way I am thinking. The way none of this is coming out right.

I so wish to touch upon everything. I live in a fantasy world. It is full of lies and I believe every single one of them. I live a selfish life. I live a guilty life. I wish to touch upon each and every one of these things. My regrets. The hatred I often feel towards myself.

But I don't know how.

I won't be able to do this ever again.

But I need to stop now. Because the dreams are tempting me. I can escape into them. Even if only for a while.

And I need to stop because, 12:13 on a Saturday morning, I am tired. Simple as that, I need sleep.

See, this is what I mean. 11:50 on a Saturday morning and I am once again sitting on my bed. My dog is with me this time.

But this is what I mean: All the pain is still there. It's balled up, clenching in my heart and stomach. But I don't know how to let it out. I don't know how to write like I just did last night.

There are so many things I want and need to talk about. I just don't know how.

My dog is sick. I don't understand sickness. Why does the world need sickness when all it causes is pain? I don't get it.

The world is horrible. I don't understand the world. How can everything be so wrong <u>all</u> the time and yet we still live in it contently? Is it simply that no one is aware of it? Or is it that everyone is so good at ignoring it, except me? I don't get it.

I don't understand people. One person — *one* — can cause so much hurt. And yet I love them anyways. So it isn't people I don't understand — it's myself.

If I don't understand *myself*, how is it that I'm supposed to understand anything else in life?

There are so many things I think about. And I can't begin to put words to them. But I want to get it all out so it stops hurting. I just don't know how.

But, you'd think, that's what I'm doing now, isn't it? Getting all of this out? I'm not. This is just the surface of things. The surface of so many levels of hurt. And I'm afraid. Because I can't seem to penetrate deeper than the surface with my words. And my words are the only things powerful enough to do it.

There's so much to say. How did I never realize there was this much to say?

"Why are you stressing?" she asked me.
Lies. Not even anyone else's.
Just my own.

Why can one thing have so many meanings? A wave. It's hello. It's goodbye. It's an ocean. Green. It's earth. It's a way of life. It's envy.

How can people understand each other when each word can mean so many things?

She scares me. She's my best friend, and she scares me. Though I guess in a way, everyone scares me.

I disgust myself. Completely and utterly disgust myself. I see myself mess up, but only after it happens. Because *that's* going to help so much.

Everything is in the present isn't it? The past was once the present. It just had to move out of the way to give the current present a turn. The future is nothing but the present waiting to happen. Once the present becomes a past present, there is room for the future present to become the present present. It's as simple as that.

So why is the past full of regrets, and the future full of fear?

I just realized something. There *is* no way to let out all of this hurt. I'm trying to get it out — to rid myself of it — but it's impossible. There's no way to do it.

I can try, and I certainly have tried, but it's hopeless.

At this point what can I do? I have to learn not to dwell on it, I guess. I have to live with it. I have to see it all so clearly in my head and find no words for it. I have to let it wash over me. Like a wave. Like that hello goodbye ocean wave.

I have to let it hurt me. Simple as that, I have to let the hurt hurt me.

I think I feel fear. Simple as that, I am afraid.

But what I am afraid of is the strange thing. I am afraid to write *this*. I am afraid to write what I am currently writing. Why? Because I fear it won't come out like it did before.

Two days ago I wrote that. Two days. That isn't such a long time. But the gap is menacing.

There is still so much to say. Though I thought it could not be done—though I still think it can't be done—I'm still going to say what I need to say. Even though I'm afraid to.

12:23 on a Monday morning and I'm going to try. Simple as that, I'm just going to try.

The ticking of a clock? It makes no sense. It isn't like it's ticking *towards* anything. It isn't like it helps anyone with anything. So why is it there?

If you just sit and listen to it, the ticking, it does nothing but scare you. It scares me. Why? Because it is almost like the seconds of my life are ticking away with each soft click.

I'm not on my bed this time. 12:27 on a Monday morning and I'm sitting in a computer chair. I'm sitting with my head against the wall.

With the clock ticking my life away.

The world? Why is it even here? Why are *we* here? Have you ever noticed there is no point to any existence? Has *no one* ever noticed that?

I mean, sure, why not make the best of it while we're here? But why we're here in the first place is what I'm wondering. We're born. We go through our lives. We die. Then what? The next generation does the same exact thing.

But nothing is ever really done in the world. Yeah, a lot of stuff happens, but nothing really *happens*. At this point, we are all doing what we do just for the sake of doing what we can do.

I don't get it.

12:33 on a Monday morning and the world makes no sense.

I think now what I feel is anger. It's bubbling up, into and through me. And it isn't even *at* anyone, or anything.

It's only there because I want to be able to write this. But I can't. Even after two days I still can't. Even though that's what I'm doing.

How can each emotion have a name? How is it that in the wide spectrum of what each individual can feel, we can classify it with a simple word? Why is "sad" what it is? Sad feels different to everyone, but it's still the same thing. Why?

I can say "I'm happy." And everyone will seem to know what I mean. But isn't happiness individual and unique to each person? So why can we make words for emotions?

12:39 on a Monday morning and I'm still here. I'm still in this computer chair, head against the wall, clock ticking away my life, wondering why the world exists.

12:40 on a Monday morning and I'm still here. Listening through the silence for footsteps, for movement, for words.

12:41 on a Monday morning and I am wondering why I keep telling the time. Am I not further counting the seconds of my life that way? Am I not showing how much time I am wasting in this life I am living (which exists for some unknown reason)?

12:43 on a Monday morning and I am still frantically trying to get rid of all this hurt. Even though I know that I cannot.

I feel fear. 12:44 on a Monday morning and simple as that, I feel fear. Again. Why? Simply because I don't want to be found here. I shouldn't even be here.

So why don't I just get up and move to my bed? I

could. But I fear doing that as well. Why? Because now that I've gotten myself started again, the gap will make me fear starting again.

But there is more fear. It is more of a panic. And I simply feel this because of how I am writing. This doesn't feel like me. This feels like it is someone else.

Yet it *is* me. And that comforts me and makes me afraid at the same time.

The real reason for this panic? This is coming out in a trance. I am writing without writing. Without thinking of writing.

Maybe it is the lack of thought that makes this so difficult. But it is an overload of thought at the same time.

My body is feeling anxiety. But my mind isn't registering it. Why? Because my mind is over exhausted. My mind is so full of all this hurt I need to rid myself of that it refuses to feel much more.

I guess in a way that is good. But in a way it scares me.

12:51 on a Monday morning and I am here. Still.

I think it is time for me to move. Though I fear not being able to continue this, I am still going to move. It's as simple as that. Get up, move, start again. So why can't I do it?

Sadness is beginning to settle in. Why? Because once again, I am tired. Simple as that, I need sleep. And my thinking is altered. This isn't coming out right. Each time I write it is different.

But maybe this is an everchanging neverending tale of hurt.

Either way, it is time for me to move.

12:55 on a Monday morning, and fear is making me move. Fatigue is making me move.

I can't be here anymore. Simple as that, I need to move.

He's running later today. Simple as that, he's running. But something feels wrong about that. Something always feels wrong about this.

Maybe it's because others die running what he is to run.

But do I really fear for his death?

Part of me fears for anyone's death. But I don't think this will kill him. It never has, it shouldn't this time, and it won't in the future.

So why don't I want him to do it? Why don't I ever want him to do it?

I didn't make it to my bed. 1:03 on a Monday morning and I made it to this table.

My thoughts have begun overflowing again. And I need to get them out while I still can. Even though I can't.

So I didn't make it past this table. 1:04 on a Monday morning and I am sitting at this table.

I think she was right. I think they were all right, when they said it.

It isn't admitting it to her that scares me. I don't know what it is that scares me. But it makes me afraid.

She may have been wrong. They may have all been wrong.

But I think they were all right.

It is time to be completely straightforward about something. What happens when I begin to talk about what I've already said? It's bound to happen at some point.

These things don't just hurt me up until I write about them. They will come back and hurt again. That letter. It still hurts.

So what happens when I begin repeating?

It will be a repetition, that's all.

Simple as that, it will be a repetition.

My mind doesn't feel like my mind sometimes. It feels like its own entity. It feels like it works without me.

And sometimes, like now, it works against me. It seems to be working so hard to make this impossible for me.

My mind feels like too much sometimes.

Sometimes I wonder if I could lose it, just for a little while.

How can here be here? Is there only one here? Or are there many? Am I in each here without knowing it?

And if I'm not in each here, then how can I say, "I am here"? That would be nothing but a lie.

1:13 on a Monday morning and I need to move. Again. Simple as that, I need to get up. Why? Because once again I shouldn't be here.

So once again the fear and sadness come. But I need to get up.

Simple as that, I need to move.

1:30 on a Monday morning and I'm In my bed again. Maybe it will end here. I started this here so why can't I end it here too? That seems as though it's the right way to do things.

My mind is still full. Full of everything that hurts.

Maybe I just need to be direct. Maybe that will ease things.

You are doing something strange to me. Something recently has changed. I let you do those things to me before. I thought I wanted you to. Maybe I still do want you to. But something is telling me I don't.

Something about you is building a great mistrust in me for all others like you. All males, that is. But I don't know why. I don't know why this is coming out of the blue.

I am afraid. I am afraid to be alone with you. Why? Because I don't know what will happen. I have ideas about what *might* happen. And I don't think I want that. And I don't think you'll listen to me when I say I don't.

Surprisingly, you are one male I do trust. I don't know why, when you keep hurting me. Maybe I hurt you too. And if I did, if I do, I am sorry. I'm so sorry that saying sorry almost seems useless.

But despite this, I feel comfortable with you. And I don't know why. I don't know why, when all other males make me so scared, you are the one who doesn't. Somehow, that hurts.

You really don't know all the things you make me feel, do you? You wouldn't even think to imagine all of these feelings, caused by you.

It's a hurt so intense that sometimes I feel it should physically wound me.

But I don't understand it. Why? Because it is a good pain. How can it hurt me so much that in the end, it's good?

I love you. You hurt me, but I love you. And amidst

all this negativity, I want to add something positive: Thank you. For everything you do. For everything you are, everything you have been, and everything you will be. For everything you are to me, thank you.

Maybe it is so much love that hurts me. Just in your case. Because you are the only thing positive within this negativity. The only thing.

We never speak anymore. Not like we used to. So how is it that after all this time, after everything that has happened, you understand my personality more than most people? How is it that you can still see me for exactly what I am, even after all this change?

But I am afraid too. I'm afraid to get on your bad side. Because I see you hurting her. After she was your friend for so long. She didn't even do what you think she did. It was all his fault and you don't see it. And because of that you've ruined everything with her. And because of that I'm afraid to ever do anything wrong around you.

I'm beginning to realize something. 1:55 on a Monday morning and I'm finally realizing something. Every person who comes into my life hurts me. That's how life goes, isn't it? People hurting people?

So obviously that's going to happen to me.

Obviously I'm going to do it to other people too.

But for some reason, now, everything they've done to hurt me—all the major things—are hurting again.

That shouldn't happen. That isn't even healthy to

happen. So why is it happening?

But maybe it's okay to at least try and let it out, if it's there. Even if it shouldn't be there.

2:00 on a Monday morning and I'm afraid. Again. Why? Because I hear movement in the house.

It isn't like she's going to open the door and speak to me. And even if she does, so?

But I'm still afraid. Maybe it's because 2:02 on a Monday morning, I'm sitting in bed.

This has made me discover something about myself. I'm afraid to make people mad. No, I'm afraid to hurt people. I am afraid that everything I do may be hurting someone.

But I can't please everyone—no one can. So why am I so afraid of something that is impossible to *not* do? Am I so afraid of losing people that I feel one small bit of hurt will get rid of them forever?

That doesn't feel right to say, but maybe it's right.

I think maybe I need to be direct again. Simple as that, I need to be direct. I think maybe, for some things, that helps more than anything else.

Then again, I am beginning to feel guilty.

But being direct may be the best choice.

I was drunk that night. Simple as that, I was drunk. And you didn't even notice. Or if you did, why didn't you say anything?

I don't even know why I did it — it wasn't an escape for once. I don't know why I didn't admit it to you right then and there . Or ever.

I didn't want you to be disappointed in me, I think. I still don't. Because I disappoint you enough as it is.

But I'm saying this now. I was drunk.

It's still you. 2:13 on a Monday morning, I'm trying to move on to the next person, and it's still you.

Do I really feel I've hurt you that much? So much that I can't even bring myself to move on to another person?

I don't even know if I *have* hurt you that much. I know I've caused pain. You've admitted to it. You've rubbed it in my face. And I apologized. Maybe you didn't think it was sincere, but I meant it. With all my heart.

I'm sorry.

Still you. I don't know why I act the way I do towards you sometimes.

But maybe I do know why.

You worry me. Sometimes the things you say, they worry me. You don't realize how what you say appears, I think. You never realize how you're acting appears either. And that worries me too.

I think my worry turns into anger. Or frustration. Why? Because I get so frustrated with myself for not being able to do anything to help you. It makes me so frustrated at myself that I get frustrated with you. And I don't know why I don't just admit that.

I just want more than anything for you to be okay. And I'm sorry for how I act because of that.

Still you. You were right. I think you always have been. And now I'm scared because I don't know what to do next.

Still you. I'm scared for you. For next year. For every year after next year. I'm scared for you because I don't know how you'll handle yourself.

And I'm scared for me because I don't know what I'm supposed to do without you.

Why have I put off mentioning you? You're the one who made all of that seem okay. Who encouraged me to continue. Even when I'd stopped.

But I guess in reality I don't blame you. It was my own stupid decision. Plus, you've changed. Which means she was right.

I guess the real reason I even need to mention you is that I'm sorry I never stopped you. I'm sorry I haven't been stopping you. I say "oh" and sit back and observe.

And that does nothing but hurt you. Even if you can't see that.

No. 2:35 on a Monday morning and it hurts. Simple as that, it hurts. Writing directly, it's not direct. Those people don't know who they are. They'll never know what they've done to me and what I've done to them.

So what's the point in saying that it's direct when in reality, it's more vague than ever?

That's just another lie.

2:38 on a Monday morning and I am sad. Why? Because this has turned into much less than I wanted it to be.

I wanted this to be powerful, and strong. But instead it is making me appear weak and feel weak.

In the end, this is all one great big weakness isn't it? All of this. Even my reason for writing is just a weakness. I'm not even writing this because I want to. I'm writing this because I need to.

I don't know who I'm talking to. This all seems to be directed towards someone, and I didn't realize that until now.

But I have no one in mind. I have someone in mind but I don't think it's her. And if it is, why?

2:43 on a Monday morning and I am still sitting on my bed. I am still listening through the silence for movement. I am still remembering. Still thinking. Still hurting. 2:45 on a Monday morning, still trying to rid myself of this hurt, and now I am physically affected.

My hand throbs, my neck aches and my eyes burn. All because of my need to rid myself of this hurt.

But still I feel myself needing to continue.

Why is it that we rely so much on technology? Why is it that we have to take advantage of the world <u>all</u> the time, just for the sake of technology?

We keep creating big new things to fix problems in the world. But those are problems we made in the first place. And then we find ourselves needing to create a big new thing to fix the problems the big new thing from before created.

Why , then, do we still find the need to create so many big new things?

And why is it that we lose interest in and forget these big new things shortly after they're created?

We're humans and we make no sense.

Simple as that, I don't understand my own kind.

Why is it that one musical note means absolutely nothing to anybody? Yet you take a string of notes, play them as a song, and everyone is moved by them?

Why can no one see an individual note for what it is? And why can no one appreciate it until it's formed something completely different?

I am growing weary. Simple as that, I'm a girl of seventeen growing weary. Why? Because I have written so much and my mind is still full.

But I am tired. 3:01 on a Monday morning and I need sleep. So though I need to rid myself of all of this, and though I still don't quite know how, I am letting myself escape into dreams. Just for a short while.

Because though my mind aches with this hurt, I am tired. Simple as that, I need sleep.

However there is one more thing. 3:09 on a Monday morning and I have discovered something.

I don't believe in myself. I believe in what I've imagined myself to be.

Now I just need to figure out how true that statement is.

And now, I am tired. Simple as that, I need sleep.

See-Saw (6/20/07)

As I teeter on the see-saw of love and death, I wonder when it will stop, where I will go, when I will go. I await the death that I am destined to meet. The electric red scars shine bright as metal again meets skin. They tell me not to go, but they don't know. They don't understand the pain awakening within me; the death falling upon me. Oh what I would give for them to just understand and let me go. So as I sit on the see-saw of life and death, I pray to land in death, that which awaits me. Why don't you understand...?

Untitled (1/ 30/07)

Forever abandoned in the sea of Loneliness
Shipwrecked on this Island of Lost Dreams
Kept in Silence through pain and Agony
Trapped with this animal inside me.
Bombarded, with red hot arrows of anger.
Lost, lost in the neverending forest of humans.
INVISIBLE.

Untitled (4/22/08)

Night by Night and
Day by Day
I ask myself if I should stay.

I cower beneath all these things
That threaten constantly as they sing.

The sun shines bright
but I don't care
I'm buried in books
with much delight.

But the pain engulfs me
as I sit and read.
As I let myself
bleed and bleed.

There are all these things
I've yet to do
And still I wonder
if I can push through

With all this help
you'd think I'd try
But still I find
I just want to die

I wish this suffering
would be gone
So I can throw it away
And just move on

But still it continues
to overpower me
Much I hide
so no one can see.

Above all that I right
Night by Night
Day by Day
I ask myself if I should stay.

It's Time to go (4/23/08)

As I stare at the clock
And the minutes slow
I finally know that
It's time to go.

I hope not to come back
but with my luck,
I know that on this world
I will be stuck.

When will Death arrive?
For I'm anxious to meet him.
As I sit and wait
On this fragile limb.

I've pushed everyone away
Even those I hold dear
I can no longer stay
It's towards death that I steer.

And as I look down
and see cuts row upon row
I finally know that
It's time to go.

Llamas (9/7/08)

I think there's a dent in my skull
Life just seems to be so dull
But I know that there will always be
LLAMAS

One day there were plumcots for sale
That sounds like a food in jail
But there will always be
LLAMAS

It's 2am and I should sleep
Sometimes water's very deep
But we will always have
LLAMAS

Sometimes I hear people snore
Most hobos are really poor
But they can always live with
LLAMAS

Gas costs so much money
That it really is quite funny
Buy you can always ride the
LLAMAS

Origami's really cool
Our president is such a fool
But we can just elect some
LLAMAS

I think this song is really lame
But who knows? It could cause fame
Because the whole thing is about
LLAMAS

In a zoo I saw a baboon
I once sat on a balloon
But I did it while looking at
LLAMAS

Well this song I think is long enough
My brain is full of purple fluff
And now you've come to love the
LLAMAS

Oh Cheese Louise (9/10/08)

The cheese climbed up the tree,
And I'm not sure how it did.
A squirrel came out to see
And the cheese just went and hid.
Finally the cheese came out
And the squirrel still sat there.
The cheese began to doubt
That it could live with a squirrel so fair.
They decided to say hello
They met out on a limb.
Turns out the cheese was made of jello
And the squirrel cut up and ate him.

Nooglemuffles and Peenyweenies

Once upon a time, in a faraway land called Pagoogaville, there lived a husband and a wife. There was Richard, generally known by his nickname Dick. His wife was named Weanna. Dick was a strongly built peenyweenie who outgrew all those his age when he was younger. Weanna, on the other hand was a delicate nooglemuffle who was often made fun of for her size as a kid. But big and small, Dick and Weanna were attracted to each other.

A year after being married they had a kid who they named Teeny, because he was in fact, a teeny peenyweenie. His size, they claimed, didn't matter to them.

"I don't care if you're small, my love," Weanna told him during one of his teenage years. "I'll love you just the same."

But still she worried.

"Oh my boy, don't you worry, you'll grow to be big and strong like your old man," said Dick.

But he too worried for his son.

They worried about his size quite a lot, in fact, because they knew that no one really loved small peenyweenies. Weanna herself fell for Dick because of his large size and worried he would never find a nooglemuffle of his own.

Teeny came to discover this for himself one day, when he finally went out looking for a nooglemuffle to call his wife.

"Hi," he said nervously to one exceptionally

beautiful nooglemuffle, "would you like to go take a swim in lake Lickinfuck?"

The nooglemuffle laughed loudly in his face.

"ME? Go out with YOU?! Look at your tiny size, you must be kidding me, surely," she said coldly to him and she walked away.

And this is what happened every time Teeny talked to a nooglemuffle.

This is hopeless, he thought. *Size really does matter.* And so he gave up his search for love.

One day, however, a new nooglemuffle by the name of Gina arrived in town, riding upon a llama and gazing adoringly out at Pagoogaville. She spotted Teeny crying by lake Lickinfuck and immediately dismounted her llama.

"Excuse me," she said cautiously to him, "but why are you crying?"

He told his story of failed love to her, staring down at the ground the whole time. When he finished he finally looked up into her face and saw that she was the most beautiful nooglemuffle he'd ever seen. And she was looking at him with care, not with hatred and disgust.

"Forget all of those nooglemuffles," she exclaimed. "You're perfect for me."

And so with a smile Teeny and Gina took a swim in Lake Lickinfuck, and then rode away on the llama into the sunset, living happily ever after.

Burning, Burning Me Away

Burning, burning me away. Fire erupting, tearing me
to shreds.
Days like this? Can we LIVE?
Everyone dies one day. Don worry your's will come.
Burning me away, fire and hatred. Blares of crowds.
LEAVE THE DEAD ALONE!
The right place, the right time. Don't be worried.
We're the death of ourselves.
Burning, burning me away.
I prayed it would go away, though more and more it
grew.
We're all dead now.
I'm dead.
Hello Death, you are welcome in my home.
Scars on my arm, just the beginning.
Next comes DEATH.
LEAVE THE DEAD ALONE!
We're at peace, yes death hello.
Come to my home and take me away, away from this
corrupted world.
Innocence doesn't exist.
I want to fucking tear myself apart.
This feels right.
Burning, burning my away.

I'm dead now, in Hell, away from this fucked up
world. Don't worry, your day will come.
The end of the Living Dead has begun
And the fire comes, burning, burning me away.

I belong to you (3/10/09)

A part of my heart
Though in many parts
Will always belong to you.

A part of my soul
Though with many holes
Will always belong to you.

A part of my mind
With much left behind
Will always belong to you.

All in all
Though I may fall
I will always belong to you.
I love you.

Untitled (3/15/10)

Drift...
Though the Earth may call, I
Drift...
Though this is where I belong, I
Drift...

Beyond who I am
Beyond anything I will be
Beyond...

I drift...Beyond this place.
Drift beyond me.
Drift...

Um.

"Close enough," I said as I put the star on the Christmas tree.

I stood back to admire my work and realized how truly lopsided my star was. And the entire tree for that matter. I laughed.

"Um mom can you possible fix the star? I kinda screwed it up. ...A lot."

My mom, who was in the process of painting her nails red and green, looked up and smiled at my horrible job. "I don't know, I think I kind of like it like that," she said.

My OCD started kicking in. "Mom seriously can you fix it?"

"That's not such a good idea," she whispered, suddenly nervous. "Plus," she added in a louder voice, "My nails are wet." She wiggled her fingers at me.

"S'okay, I'll wait," and I plopped sideways onto the couch and watched my mother. She still looked nervous but I decided not to question it.

She continued to paint her nails. I looked closely and realized she was taking a really long time to paint her nails and putting so much more effort into it than usual.

"Mom. Any day now."

"Right," she said frantically and finished up.

We talked as we waited for her nails to dry. Finally, they did.

"Well?" I demanded. "The star?"

"I don't know, your father usually..."

But my father had died just a few months before of a rare liver disease.

Softly I said, "It's fine though, I'm sure you're perfectly capable of doing just as good a job as he would've."

"Fine," she said with a deep breath, getting nervous again. "I guess this is inevitable. It was bound to happen someday."

"What—"

But she had already climbed the ladder. She reached to (finally) fix the star and when she grabbed it...

She turned into a llama

The End.

The Schizophrenic Lullaby

Hush little Voices, don't say a word.
If anyone hears you, they'll think I'm absurd.

If they think I'm absurd then the men will come,
Wearing all white and holding a gun.

And if they aim their guns at me,
I'll yell and scream and fall to my knees.

And if I fall they'll take me away,
Though I tried to keep You at bay.

So Voices, leave, don't let them hear,
You're making me live a life of fear.

This life of fear, You'll be sad to see,
Will be the end of You and the end of me.

So if You want to stay just know
I'll end this life if You don't lay low.

Insanity

Even in Nothing, I taste. I smell. I feel.
Even in Quiet, I hear.
Even in Blackness, I see.

In the Darkness I lie, crying, screaming, fighting.
In the Darkness I run, searching for escape.

Running and Hiding.
From the World.
From Myself.
From Everything.

From Nothing.

It's all in my Head.

Falling

All is falling, inside and out.

Falling and Failing,
Unbearably.
Crying,
Kicking, fighting.

In silence and darkness,
Teetering on the edge.

Alone.
Longing.
Lost.

All is falling, inside and out.

It's all a lie.

Untitled

The rain is dripping
Slowly dropping
Drip Drop
Drip Drop.

The thunder is booming
Loudly Crashing
Boom Crash
Boom Crash.

My soul is crying
Greatly lying
Run Fall
Run Fall.

Untitled

Page after page
Line after line
WAITING, waiting to be filled

Thought after thought
Pain after pain
WAITING, waiting to release.

Combine, mix
Fill, release?
No.

Hey.

I have the most amazing friends.

I have a giant family (mainly on my mom's side — she's Portuguese) and I love every member of it.

I sort of go to the University of Massachusetts Amherst, where I'm currently studying Psychology (I'm on medical leave and don't know when I'm going back. I also may switch my major, or colleges even.)

I care about others and want to work in a mental hospital.

I work at McDonald's. It doesn't sound great, but it isn't so bad. And hey, at least it's a job.

I volunteer at the local animal shelter.

I also work at an animal sanctuary, mainly in the cat house.

I'm an animal lover, and tend to like *them* more than I like people.

People tell me I'm kind and caring, a great friend and a good writer.

Making me smile is fairly easy.

I've helped others to get the courage to go to therapy and become happier people. I've helped them smile through their tears, and have hugged their pain away.

But despite all of that...

I have bipolar disorder.

And anxiety.

And depression.

And OCD.

And an eating disorder.

I hate everything about myself.

Most of the time, I feel like I don't even know myself.

I don't like the way I look. In fact, I basically hate it.

I've struggled with my weight my whole life, being told year after year by my doctor that I need to lose weight and I've never seemed to be able to do so.

I have a tendency to resort to cutting when things get to be too overwhelming.

I've turned to drugs and alcohol in the past.

I replay things in my head constantly, to an overwhelming extent.

I hide my pain from everyone. When I'm smiling, chances are I'm screaming or crying on the inside.

I've gone to a mental hospital and may end up in one again sometime in the future, if not multiple times.

I always put everyone before myself and suffer because of it.

I'm bisexual and though my family knows, I often wonder if they truly accept me.

Basically I'm a mess.

I have all of these good things going for me. I'd even say I'm lucky because I have so many positive things in my life. But I'm falling apart, and have been for years—learning, as I said, to smile and laugh on the outside even though inside I'm screaming, crying and suffering.

How the hell did I end up like this?

Change

Is this how it ends, then? Surely not, surely there has to be some way to save the day, and with it, all of humanity?

But if not then it must be time for last goodbyes. I Love you, and you, and you too, goodbye, goodbye, goodbye.

Llama Drama

Once upon a time there was a llama. And what a fine llama she was. This llama, Shnigglenama had a mother, a father and a little brother, Doonama. This fine llama loved her mother and father dearly but found Doonama to be quite annoying and always in her way, not to mention all her parents' attention was on him all the time which she hated.

One day Shnigglenama Llama was playing with her toys. To be more specific, she was playing with her porcelain alpacas, having a tea party. What was even more exciting is that her parents let her use actual tea this time. *They finally trust me!* she thought, glad that her parents knew that unlike her stupid brother, she was old enough to do grown up things like have a real tea party.

While she was in her room conversing with Sacka, her favorite alpaca, in came Doonama with a smile on his face.

"Ew what do you want?" asked Shnigglenama with disgust.

Completely ignorant of her tone, Doonama asked, "Can I please join in your tea party? It looks like a lot of fun. And look! I brought my own guest!" He held up a stuffed animal. It was a pony.

"No. And this is a party for *alpacas* not disgusting and smelly *horses*."

"Aw, please? I'll be careful," he pleaded.

Before she could tell him no again, he had run

over to the little pink table, placed his pony (named Coney) in an empty seat and sat himself in another empty chair. He placed a teacup in front of Coney. Realizing there was nothing she could to do get him out, Shnigglenama sighed and approached the table. Just as she was about to sit, Doonama went to grab the teapot and dropped it on Sacka the porcelain alpaca who immediately shattered. Shnigglenama froze for a moment. Then she exploded with rage.

"WHAT DID YOU DO?! I HATE YOU!" she screamed at him.

Doonama stared at her in shock then ran out of the room crying. *Good,* she thought with amusement at his pathetic tears. Then she glanced at her broken friend and shed a few tears of her own. Suddenly she heard the front door slam.

She ran downstairs to the living room where her parents were both getting up in shock and fear and asked what the slam was. No one knew until they realized...

Doonama wasn't there.

They ran around the house calling his name but he was nowhere to be found—he had run away from home.

Guilt engulfed Shnigglenma. This was all her fault. And she realized something—she was really scared for her brother. She actually loved him! But she didn't know how that would possibly help to get him back.

She and her parents hopped in their purple llama-mobile and began driving around the neighborhood, calling Doonama's name out the window and asking all those they passed whether they'd seen him (they hadn't) and to please keep an eye out for him.

It started to rain.

They searched and searched but had no idea where poor little Doonama had gone.

"Maybe he's back at home already?" mother llama suggested, so they headed back home quickly.

He wasn't there. But they figured that before calling the police, they would wait it out a bit and see if Doonama would find his way home. They waited.

And waited.

And waited some more.

Just as father llama picked up the phone to finally call the police, the doorbell rang.

Everyone ran to the door and mother llama threw it open. Alas, there was Doonama, looking so sad with tears still in his eyes, soaking wet and...

Holding a package?

He immediately handed it to Shnigglenama who stared at it in confusion. Then slowly she opened the wet package. Inside was a brand new porcelain alpaca, very similar to Sacka. It even had the same color dress.

"I felt bad for breaking your favorite toy, so I went and bought a new one with all the money in my piggy bank. I know it isn't the same but I wanted to try and make it better...." Doonama said timidly to Shnigglenama, waiting for another outburst.

Shnigglenama looked at the alpaca for a moment then handed it off to her mother. She hugged her brother.

"I don't care about any stupid toys. As long as I

have you, I'm happy. I love you Doonama."

They smiled at each other.

"Now," she said, "who's ready for a tea party?"

The End

Help me, Save me.

Pain, pain, go away
Come again another day.
Or rather, don't, ever again,
So far you have come with no end.

But please really, leave,
All I need is relief.
I can't do this anymore,
Oh god, what's in store?

I'm drowning, falling
And oh Death is calling
But if you'd go away...
Please, please I pray.

I'm grasping, reaching
And Death keeps on preaching
Pulling me in,
Replaying my sins.

I see and I listen
About to give in
I'm about to fail
I'm far too frail

I'm through, I'm done
I'll continue to run
I need you
But I'm hiding too.

Don't let me go
Don't let the pain flow
Help me, save me.
Help me, save me.

Except...

I did it, I failed you.
I swear this is true.
The blood on my wrists
Is a sure sign of this.

Please kill me, destroy me,
I can't believe me.
The pain that I bring,
The pain lingering.

The guilt and the shame
The hurt and the blame,
It's all because of me.
Please why can't you see?

I tried not to do this
Tried finding some bliss
But I let the pain erupt
God why did I fuck up?

You stayed, you tried,
You saw through my lies.
You're everything to me,
You begged and you plead.

But do I listen? No.
I let the pain flow.
And I didn't tell you
Though that'd be the right thing to do.

I keep hiding, denying
Yet you keep on spying
And I'm sorry, I am
For everything, goddamn.

But I need to be true,
Be honest to you.
I completely screwed up
And fucked my life up.

I did it, I failed you
I swear this is true.
The blood on my wrists,
They're a sure sign of this.

⎯⎯⎯❈⎯⎯⎯

Oh shit

"Rhythm of Love" began blaring out of nowhere and I jumped in fright. The man with the knife looked around in confusion and I glanced down at the chains on my arms and legs, in the hopes that they would just disappear, that all of this would disappear and not be happening. Where was this music coming from? I had no more time to consider this thought as a knife was plunged into my chest. I cried out in pain...

Then I woke up. Rhythm of Love continued playing on my phone and I turned the alarm off. My heart was racing and tears welled up in my eyes. I tried to shake off the dream but couldn't help replaying all of it and most of all remembering the feeling of the knife as it had entered my chest. I sat up in bed and looked around, searching for comfort. I hugged my teddy bear, which as a 19 year old girl I still slept with. Eventually, no less traumatized, I managed to at least stop shaking.

Looking back at my phone, I noticed six texts from two of my friends. *How come those couldn't have woken me up from my nightmare before it got bad?* I sleepily responded to them, slid my phone shut and squirmed out of bed. One deep breath later it suddenly hit me.

The interview.

I had an interview that day at Target, in the hopes that someone would finally hire me. I wasn't getting my hopes up *too* high though—I'd already applied so many other places without a single response. Maybe (hopefully) this time I'd be lucky.

I walked over to the closet. Black skinny jeans and my nice grey striped sweater. Nice enough for a Target interview? Hopefully, seeing as that's where I bought the clothes in the first place. I laughed as I put my bra, underwear and socks on the bed with the clothes. Their obnoxiously bright colors contrasted so much with my shirt and jeans. *Good thing they won't be seeing those.*

I carried it all into the bathroom. I went through my routine—brush my teeth, brush my hair, put on deodorant, put on clothes. I looked down at myself, not liking what I saw. Then I looked in the mirror. *Maybe they'll take one look at me and decide they don't want me.* I couldn't help thinking that. I'd had issues with my appearance since the sixth grade. Continuing to look in the mirror, I stared at all the details on my face—my messy blonde hair, my boring grey eyes, large nose, weird ears, big eyebrows, small lips. Disgusting. Looking away, I grabbed my phone which I'd brought with me as well and headed to the kitchen for breakfast. My mom had made waffles for the occasion and I buried myself in its doughty syrupy goodness before checking the time.

"It's 11:30, my interview's at 12," I told my mom. "I should leave and be early. Right? They like if you're early, right? 'Cause if not, I mean, I could wait a bit and show up, I don't know, but—"

My mom laughed at my nervousness. "Just go. I'll clean up."

"Okay, thanks mom."

I started heading out the door then realized I didn't have my shoes, keys or jacket. *Wow, stupid much?* Two or three minutes later, I had everything I needed,

including my wallet which I'd also forgotten and head-
ed out the door.

The drive there calmed me down a lot. Music blar-
ing, the sense of freedom...it was great. But once I
reached the parking lot, parked my car and turned it
off my nervousness and anxiety came rushing back in
the silence.

Just. Go. In.

I actually listened to myself and got out of the car.
The door slammed shut and the sounds seemed louder
than usual. There was a roaring in my ears. There were
so many people. *Are they all looking at me? Oh my god
they know I have an interview, they know I'm not going to
get hired, is that girl making fun of me?* I tried tuning out
my thoughts, and didn't succeed. But I headed inside
anyway.

Once inside, the smell of the store hit me and I
smiled. *I'd love working here.* That's when I realized I
had no idea where I was supposed to go. *Shit.* Standing
there probably looking really stupid, I looked around
and to make things that much worse, tears started
forming in my eyes again.

"Can I help you with something?" came a friendly
voice from behind me.

I swiveled around to find a guy around my parents'
age looking at me. He was skinny with greying brown-
ish hair and a Target uniform on. There was something
strange and vague about the way he was looking at
me. Was it anger? Whatever, I was clearly imagining
things. I looked at his name tag. Nathaniel.

"Yeah um, interview. I have yeah. That," I choked

out stupidly.

Nathaniel laughed. "Okay hold on I'll get the manager, okay? Wait here."

And just like that he disappeared. I stood there shaking, waiting for him to return. A minute or two later he reappeared with a huge muscular man who had greasy black hair and a giant smile on his face. Immediately he held out his hand and said "Hi! My name is Barry, are you ready for your interview?" .

I smiled back, acting as though I felt perfectly comfortable. My voice deceived me as I said in a small voice "Yes."

"Don't worry, it's not that bad," he said kindly.

He started leading me towards the back of the store. Past the electronics, clothes and food. Nathaniel tagged along which I thought was kind of strange.

"Um is this where you normally hold interviews?" I asked curiously.

"No," Barry admitted, "But my office is being used by one of the other managers at the moment so we're heading back here.

That made sense. I looked around and discovered Nathaniel had finally disappeared. Just when I thought we'd have our interview sitting by the cosmetics, a door entered my field of vision. We went through it and entered...

The storage room. *What the hell?* I had no idea interviews could be held in a storage room and my confusion outweighed my anxiety which was a bit of a shock. We continued past boxes and boxes of stuff to another door. My confusion increased and then we went through the door and there was nothing but a white van. We were outside.

"What, where—"

But my question was cut short as Barry turned around and punched me in the stomach. The pain was indescribable. A canvas bag was thrown over my head and I felt Barry pick me up and throw me. I'm assuming I was thrown into the van but I had no time to question it because I hit my head and passed out.

When I woke up my head and stomach were throbbing. My insides felt like they'd been punched too. I reached up to touch my throbbing head. Or I tried to anyway. That's when I discovered my hands had been tied together. Memories of my nightmare came flooding back and fear pulsed through me. My heart raced so fast that it hurt and my body tingled, wishing to flee but unable to do so. My feet were tied too. My mind was racing to the point where I couldn't even pinpoint any of my thoughts. I finally decided to look at my surroundings.

I was in a house. A kitchen to be more specific. The house was really nice and really modern. The kitchen was all stainless steel and marble. There was even a basket of fruit on the small island in the middle of the room and a small oak table in the corner where there sat Barry. I figured out I was sitting against the fridge.

I couldn't even speak. I couldn't function and all I could feel was fear. Fear made me forget about my injuries.

"So. You're finally awake," Barry said in a surprisingly harsh tone. "I've been waiting for a very long time."

Yeah, as if I could control how long I was passed out. I still couldn't speak.

"Aw, little Melinda is too scared to speak, huh?" he said in a mocking tone.

Stupidly I nodded. How did he even know my name? The pain in my head suddenly made me dizzy and my vision went black for a moment. He laughed. His laugh sent a chill all the way down my spine and throughout my body. It wasn't even that his laugh was disturbing. It was just disturbing coming from this smiley man who may or may not have even been a manager at Target.

Barry stood up. My pulsing fear increased as I saw he was carrying a gun. He looked down at it.

"Oh, no, this gun isn't necessary unless you don't give me what I want."

"What" I choked out quietly.

"Oh I think you know exactly what. You have something of mine and I really need it. Now."

"N-no. What." Confusion was added to my fear.

He ran up to me and grabbed my hair, pulling it up and back painfully. The throbbing in my head increased.

"Give me what I want or the pain you feel now will feel like a mere bruise. GIVE IT TO ME NOW, WHERE THE HELL IS IT?"

I shrank back in fear but suddenly found my voice. "What are you talking about?"

"'What are you talking about'" he mocked me. "You know full well what I'm talking about. No? Fine. Nathaniel, bring her in."

Nathaniel? What the hell does he have to do with any of this? Whatever this even is...

Nathaniel came charging in with an angry smile on his face. But it wasn't just him. He was dragging a girl behind him by her ankles. She was tied up too. And it wasn't just any girl.

"*RILEY!*" I cried out. My best friend of eight years, trapped here just like me. How did this happen? "What are you doing to her? Let her go."

Nathaniel dropped her just out of reach from me and she stared at me, too scared to say anything. She was crying. All we could do was stare at each other and I began to cry too. All the tears I'd been holding back all day finally came pouring out.

"You're pathetic," Nathaniel said and he kicked me in the stomach. I fell over. All this pain was unbearable.

Barry grabbed Nathaniel's arm and pulled him back. "No. She might cooperate if we don't cause her more pain." Then he looked at Riley. "And also if *this* girl's life is at stake."

"No! No no please what do you want from me?" I said through my tears.

"What do we *want* from you?" Barry kicked Riley's foot and she shrank back in fear. "We want the money you promised us."

Confusion suddenly outweighed my fear. "Um. What money?" I literally had no idea what this man was talking about.

"YOU KNOW WHAT FUCKING MONEY I'M TALKING ABOUT!" He hit Riley in the head with his gun, just hard enough to make her bleed but not hard enough to knock her out. She cried out.

"Stop," I cried even more. "Just stop hurting her, I don't have any money. I don't even know who you are."

Nathaniel suddenly looked bored and went to sit at the table. He grabbed an apple from the basket on the island and began chewing it loudly.

Barry on the other hand, after a disgusted look at Nathaniel, kneeled in front of me and put his face mere inches away from mine. "You give me my fucking money or she dies." He pointed at Riley with his gun. She started crying even more and gave me a significant look. I didn't know what it meant.

"Seriously, what money?"

"STOP SAYING THAT. Fine. Fine. HA." He pointed his gun at Riley and looked back at me.

"I love you. And I'm sorry. I'm so so sorry," Riley finally managed to say.

But sorry for what I never found out because a shockingly loud bang later, she fell over on the kitchen floor and blood very slowly began pooling around her.

"No," I sobbed. "No."

Barry smiled gleefully with an insane look in his eyes. "She's gone, bitch. Now give me what I want or you die too."

"I don't *have* what you want."

And a loud bang later, everything went black and slowly and painfully my life drained and faded away from me.

I tried...But Failed

Is it okay if I fall?
Is it okay if you call
And I don't answer the phone?
Cuz I just feel alone.

Is it okay if I drown?
Cuz when you're not around
I can't do a thing
I just keep failing

Can you see my pain,
How my life has drained?
Can I do nothing right?
I keep putting up a fight.

A fight with no one but me
That you can probably see
So you continue reaching out
You don't know what it's about

Constant failing
Constant bailing
With no words to explain
This amount of pain.

I don't want to try
I can't even cry
Feel nothing at all
Yet I continue to fall.

This is all just confusion
But it's really a fusion
Of fear and shame
Of guilt and blame.

I wish I could say
Why I feel this way
But I won't and I can't
It's a pointless rant.

And this, I see
Does not explain me,
Though I wish that it would
I wish that it could.

I just want you to know
That I'm letting go
I can't do this
I'll take the risk.

I fail, I give up
I'm getting fucked up
And I don't even care
Not even aware

That this may hurt you
But I don't know what to do
I don't know where to turn
I just want to burn.

It was always my hope
That I'd learn how to cope
But I continue to lie
I don't even try.

And you say that I won't go through with this
You say that it's me you're going to miss.
I just wish I was enough
I wish I could be tough

But I'm numb and I'm weak
And I can't even speak
I need the release
I need this to cease.

Wow here I am, just going on
Ranting, rambling, all along
All stupid fucking pointless shit
Why do you put up with it?

I wish that this could
And I wish that this would
Cover what's going on
Cover what's really wrong.

I sit here and try not to lie
Make truth of what I denied
But you can see it's done nothing
I'm trapped in an endless ring

And all this pain
God I'm insane
I'm sorry, I am
That my life is a sham

Just take a look at me
Trying to make you see
And I'm failing again
My message won't send

And...I'm in love with you
I swear that it's true
But I'm done, that's it
I can't take this shit

I admit I'm in pain
I admit I'm insane
I'm done with this lie
Goodbye, goodbye.

Recovery

When I fell asleep last night
I slipped into a dream
It gave me quite a fright,
A nightmare it would seem.

I flew above the clouds
As majestic as a hawk
I flew above the crowds
And landed on a dock.

And on that dock I thought there'd be
Many people around
But suddenly I could see
It was a monster that I found.

This monster had big red eyes
And menacing huge claws
He was eating a bowl of flies
And pointing out my flaws.

Suddenly I saw something
Lying on the ground
I thought it was a metal ring
But it was a razor blade I found.

It was then I felt my mood plummet
And though I should have let it go,
I know I shouldn't have done it
But I let the blood flow.

I held it in my hand
And after I used it
I found myself sitting in the sand
And yelled "Why, oh shit!"

Then suddenly I awoke
On my arm there was an itch
And when I finally spoke
I decided my life was just a glitch.

Just a waste of space
Just nothing it would seem
My mind's running a race
And I've run out of steam.

So it's time to finally end it
Let go and get better
I know it'll take a bit
The new me, I finally met her.

I know I can succeed
At leaving the depression hive
A happier life I will lead
And I'm glad to be alive.

Acknowledgments

Thank you first of all to Outskirts Press Inc. for helping me to succeed in my dream of publishing a book. And a special thanks to Tinamarie Ruvalcaba for helping me one on one with my book.

To keep this short, thank you to my family, my girlfriend and my friends for supporting me and being there for me through everything, and most of all for encouraging me to follow my dream. You guys make life worth living and I appreciate every second of it.

And last of all I want to thank all of you who are reading this, for giving my book a chance and for getting to know me. For those of you struggling, get help and maybe someday you'll have a tale to tell like mine.

Thank you.

CPSIA information can be obtained at www.ICGtesting.com
Printed in the USA
BVOW041956050313

314792BV00002B/128/P